# WELCOME!

## Sit Back & Relax

# THIS BOOK BELONGS TO

# Grounding Yourself

Today's Date ______________________

What is your name? ______________________

Where are you?

Words that describe your space

Who is with you? What are they doing?

Words that describe your feelings

What do you hear?

What do you see?

What can you smell?

What can you touch?

When you are calm, set an intention:

# GROUNDING

Goals

Bucket List

Inspirational
Quotes

Money

Relationship

Wellbeing

Career / Education

# VISION BOARD

Thank You For

Date

Personal Challenges

People To Pray For

Society And Government

Reflections

# GRATITUDE LOG

**Strain**

Grower

Date

Acquired $

| Indica | Hybrid | Sativa |

☐ Flower   ☐ Edible   ☐ Concentrate

## Symptoms Relieved

Sweet

Fruity   Floral

Sour   Spicy

Earthy   Herbal

Woodsy

## Notes

| Effects | Strength |

Peaceful ◯ ◯ ◯ ◯ ◯

Sleepy ◯ ◯ ◯ ◯ ◯

Pain Relief ◯ ◯ ◯ ◯ ◯

Hungry ◯ ◯ ◯ ◯ ◯

Uplifted ◯ ◯ ◯ ◯ ◯

Creative ◯ ◯ ◯ ◯ ◯

**Ratings** ☆ ☆ ☆ ☆ ☆

# CANNABIS LIST

Stop stressing about...

Ideas

Conversations

Shopping list

- 
- 
- 
- 
- 
- 
- 
- 
- 

Things to do

Explore and learn about...

# BRAIN DUMP

# MIND MAP

**Playlist Title**

Dedicated to                                                                          Date

| Song Name | Artist | Year | Notes |
| --- | --- | --- | --- |
|  |  |  |  |
|  |  |  |  |
|  |  |  |  |
|  |  |  |  |
|  |  |  |  |
|  |  |  |  |
|  |  |  |  |
|  |  |  |  |
|  |  |  |  |
|  |  |  |  |
|  |  |  |  |
|  |  |  |  |
|  |  |  |  |
|  |  |  |  |

URL

Notes

# MUSIC PLAY LIST

Date

Source of Anxiety

Time

Physical Sensations

Place

## Negative Beliefs

| About Yourself | About Situation |
|---|---|
| | |

## What facts do you know are true?

| About Yourself | About Situation |
|---|---|
| | |

Color where you feel
sensations of anxiety

## Is there a more balanced way to think about this situation

## What has helped before?

## What is helping now?

## Coping Mechanisms

Breathe
Remind yourself that anxiety is just a feeling
Describe your surroundings in detail
Go outdoors
Sip a warm or iced drink slowly
Ground yourself

# ANXIETY LOG

## Today's Goal _______________     Ⓜ Ⓣ Ⓦ Ⓣ Ⓕ ⬤ ⬤

Muscle Group Focus _______________     Weight _______     Date/Time _______

Stretch ◯     Warm-Up _______________

## Strength Training

| Exercise | | Set 1 | Set 2 | Set 3 | Set 4 | Set 5 | Set 6 |
|---|---|---|---|---|---|---|---|
| | Reps | | | | | | |
| | Weight | | | | | | |
| | Reps | | | | | | |
| | Weight | | | | | | |
| | Reps | | | | | | |
| | Weight | | | | | | |
| | Reps | | | | | | |
| | Weight | | | | | | |
| | Reps | | | | | | |
| | Weight | | | | | | |
| | Reps | | | | | | |
| | Weight | | | | | | |
| | Reps | | | | | | |
| | Weight | | | | | | |
| | Reps | | | | | | |
| | Weight | | | | | | |
| | Reps | | | | | | |
| | Weight | | | | | | |

## Cardio

| Exercise | Calories | Distance | Time |
|---|---|---|---|
| | | | |
| | | | |

Water Intake

Cooldown

Feeling ☆ ☆ ☆ ☆ ☆

## Notes

WORKOUT JOURNAL

|  | Mon | Tue | Wed | Thu | Fri | Sat | Sun |
|---|---|---|---|---|---|---|---|
| Bedtime |  |  |  |  |  |  |  |
| Time Fell Asleep |  |  |  |  |  |  |  |
| Daily Energy Level |  |  |  |  |  |  |  |
| Last Thing Eaten |  |  |  |  |  |  |  |
| Medication |  |  |  |  |  |  |  |
| Last Activity |  |  |  |  |  |  |  |
| Woke refreshed? |  |  |  |  |  |  |  |

## Chart of Hours Slept

|  | Mon | Tue | Wed | Thu | Fri | Sat | Sun |
|---|---|---|---|---|---|---|---|
| 7pm |  |  |  |  |  |  |  |
| 8pm |  |  |  |  |  |  |  |
| 9pm |  |  |  |  |  |  |  |
| 10pm |  |  |  |  |  |  |  |
| 11pm |  |  |  |  |  |  |  |
| 12pm |  |  |  |  |  |  |  |
| 1am |  |  |  |  |  |  |  |
| 2am |  |  |  |  |  |  |  |
| 3am |  |  |  |  |  |  |  |
| 4am |  |  |  |  |  |  |  |
| 5am |  |  |  |  |  |  |  |
| 6am |  |  |  |  |  |  |  |
| 7am |  |  |  |  |  |  |  |
| 8am |  |  |  |  |  |  |  |
| 9am |  |  |  |  |  |  |  |
| 10am |  |  |  |  |  |  |  |
| 11am |  |  |  |  |  |  |  |

# SLEEP TRACKER

| **Wine Name** | | |
| --- | --- | --- |
| Winery | Region | |
| Grapes | Vintage | Alcohol % |

| | | |
| --- | --- | --- |
| Appearance | | ☆ ☆ ☆ ☆ ☆ |
| Aroma | | ☆ ☆ ☆ ☆ ☆ |
| Body | | ☆ ☆ ☆ ☆ ☆ |
| Taste | | ☆ ☆ ☆ ☆ ☆ |
| Finish | | ☆ ☆ ☆ ☆ ☆ |

| Pairs With | Serving Temperature |
| --- | --- |
| | |

Notes

**Ratings** ☆ ☆ ☆ ☆ ☆

# WINE REVIEW

# Letting Go
## Self Criticism

Critical Thought

"I should..."
"I can't believe..."
"I wish..."
"I'm so stupid"

What triggered this thought?

"I was late to the meeting"
"I forgot to call my mom"
"My friend stood me up"

Physical and Emotional Sensations

How does this thought
make you feel?

Compassionate Thought

What you might say if a
friend expressed this
thought

A year from now

How will you feel about
this event next year?
Will it matter?

Concrete Plan

What action can you
take to prepare for
this in future.

Big picture plan

Imagine a future free
from this thought.
What will you do?

# BE KIND TO YOURSELF

# Finger Labyrinth

Use your finger to slowly trace a path to the center of the labyrinth

Breathe calmly and slowly as you focus.
When you reach the center, draw a long deep breath or two.

Then trace your path back to the outside
Repeat until you feel more focused and calm.

**Focus Words**

Breathe - Peace - Relax - Tranquility - Serenity - Calm - Space - Beauty
Love - Wonder - Kindness - Light - Happiness - Joy - Warmth

**Observations**

# FINGER LABYRINTH

# Happy Memory Clouds

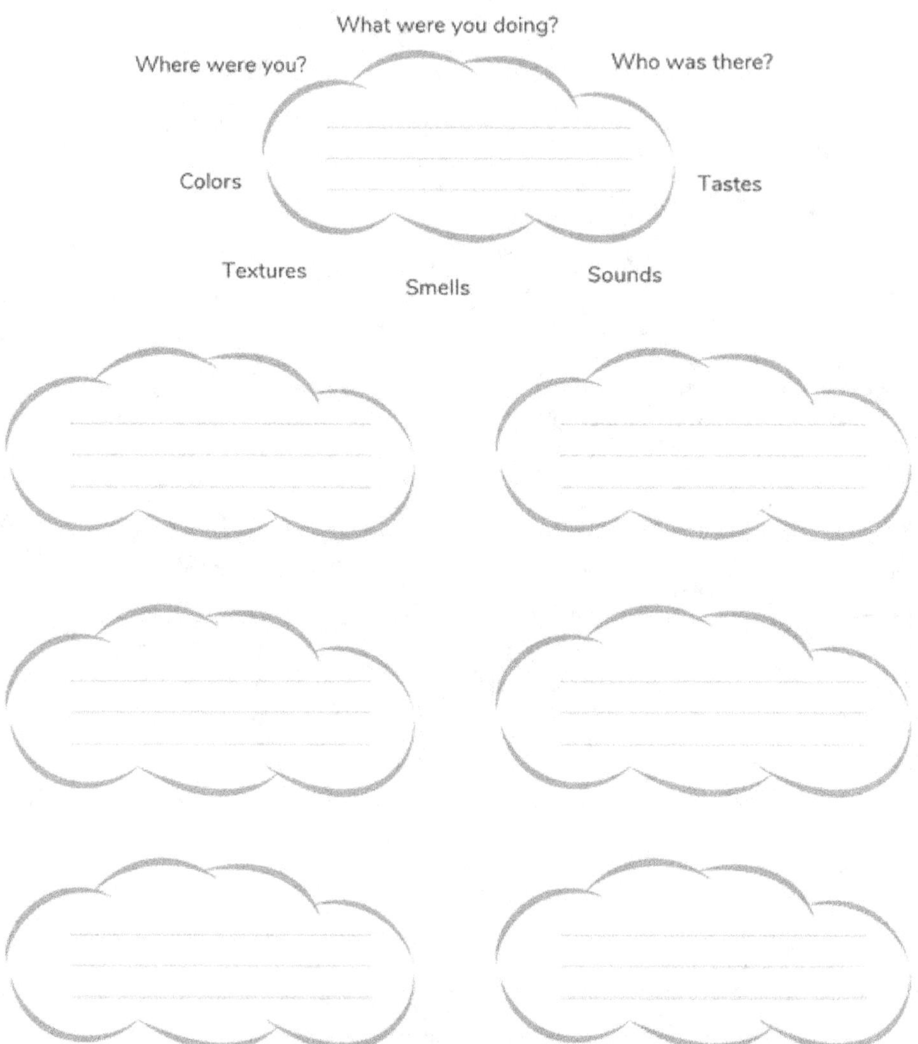


Fill out these clouds as you think of happy memories.
Use them when your emotions become overwhelming.

# HAPPY MEMORY CLOUDS

# Self Care Routine



Vision

| Time | Step |
| --- | --- |
|  |  |
|  |  |
|  |  |
|  |  |

### Routine Notes

Food

Spiritual

Exercise

Mantra

## Daily Tracker

| 1 | 2 | 3 | 4 | 5 | 6 | 7 | 8 | 9 | 10 |
| --- | --- | --- | --- | --- | --- | --- | --- | --- | --- |
| 11 | 12 | 13 | 14 | 15 | 16 | 17 | 18 | 19 | 20 |
| 21 | 22 | 23 | 24 | 25 | 26 | 27 | 28 | 29 | 30 |

MY ROUTINE

# A Safe Space

Title of space

Sketch your safe space here

Words that describe your space

Sounds

Sights

Smells

Textures

People and
animals present

A SAFE PLACE

**Book Title**

Author

Nationality

Genre

Year

Pages

| Memorable Quote | Page Number |
| --- | --- |
|  |  |
|  |  |
|  |  |
|  |  |
|  |  |

Characters

Plot Summary

Notes

**Rating** ☆ ☆ ☆ ☆ ☆

# BOOK REVIEW

Date __________    Time __________

Location __________

Telescope __________

Sky Conditions __________

Object __________

Finder

## Field Drawing

Low Power

High Power

| Eyepiece: | Mag: |
|-----------|------|
| Filter: | FOV: |

| Eyepiece: | Mag: |
|-----------|------|
| Filter: | FOV: |

## Notes

# TRACKING THE NIGHT SKY

# Habit Tracker

Month

Year

Day

1
2
3
4
5
6
7
8
9
10
11
12
13
14
15
16
17
18
19
20
21
22
23
24
25
26
27
28
29
30
31

HABIT TRACKER

Key Objective

Goal Checklist

Places to Visit

People to Meet

Notes

# GOAL CKECK LIST

# Weekly Gratitude Journal

Sunday __________
1. ______________________
   ______________________
2. ______________________
   ______________________
3. ______________________
   ______________________

Monday __________
1. ______________________
   ______________________
2. ______________________
   ______________________
3. ______________________
   ______________________

Tuesday __________
1. ______________________
   ______________________
2. ______________________
   ______________________
3. ______________________
   ______________________

Wednesday __________
1. ______________________
   ______________________
2. ______________________
   ______________________
3. ______________________
   ______________________

Thursday __________
1. ______________________
   ______________________
2. ______________________
   ______________________
3. ______________________
   ______________________

Friday __________
1. ______________________
   ______________________
2. ______________________
   ______________________
3. ______________________
   ______________________

Saturday __________
1. ______________________
2. ______________________
3. ______________________



# WEEKLY JOURNAL

STORY JOURNAL

Date

### Breakfast

| Time | Items | Serving | Cals | Sugar | Protein | Fiber | Carbs | Fat |
|------|-------|---------|------|-------|---------|-------|-------|-----|
|      |       |         |      |       |         |       |       |     |
|      |       |         |      |       |         |       |       |     |
|      |       |         |      |       |         |       |       |     |
|      |       |         |      |       |         |       |       |     |

### Lunch

| Time | Items | Serving | Cals | Sugar | Protein | Fiber | Carbs | Fat |
|------|-------|---------|------|-------|---------|-------|-------|-----|
|      |       |         |      |       |         |       |       |     |
|      |       |         |      |       |         |       |       |     |
|      |       |         |      |       |         |       |       |     |
|      |       |         |      |       |         |       |       |     |

### Dinner

| Time | Items | Serving | Cals | Sugar | Protein | Fiber | Carbs | Fat |
|------|-------|---------|------|-------|---------|-------|-------|-----|
|      |       |         |      |       |         |       |       |     |
|      |       |         |      |       |         |       |       |     |
|      |       |         |      |       |         |       |       |     |
|      |       |         |      |       |         |       |       |     |

### Snacks

| Time | Items | Serving | Cals | Sugar | Protein | Fiber | Carbs | Fat |
|------|-------|---------|------|-------|---------|-------|-------|-----|
|      |       |         |      |       |         |       |       |     |
|      |       |         |      |       |         |       |       |     |
|      |       |         |      |       |         |       |       |     |
|      |       |         |      |       |         |       |       |     |

### Total

| Serving | Cals | Sugar | Protein | Fiber | Carbs | Fat |
|---------|------|-------|---------|-------|-------|-----|
|         |      |       |         |       |       |     |

# FOOD LOG

Recipe: _______________________

Serving: ___________        Prep Time: ___________

Cook Time: ___________      Temperature: ___________

Ingredients:                Methods:

Wine Pairing: ___________________________

From the Kitchen of: _____________________

# RECIPE PLANNER

| **Plant Name** | **Date Planted** |
| --- | --- |
|  |  |

Water Requirements 💧  💧💧  💧💧💧

Sunlight ☀ ☀ ⬤

☐ Seed  ☐ Transplant

| Date | Event |
| --- | --- |
|  |  |
|  |  |
|  |  |
|  |  |
|  |  |
|  |  |

**Notes**

**Outcome**

**Uses**

Purchased at: _______________________  Price: _______________________

# GARDEN PLANNER

## Soap Name

Yield _______ Date _______

Process _______ Mold _______ Temp _______

Packaging _______

Visual Description

Fragrance Description

## Lyes and Liquids

| Name | Quantity |
| --- | --- |

## Oils

## Additives

Notes

# SOAP RECIPE

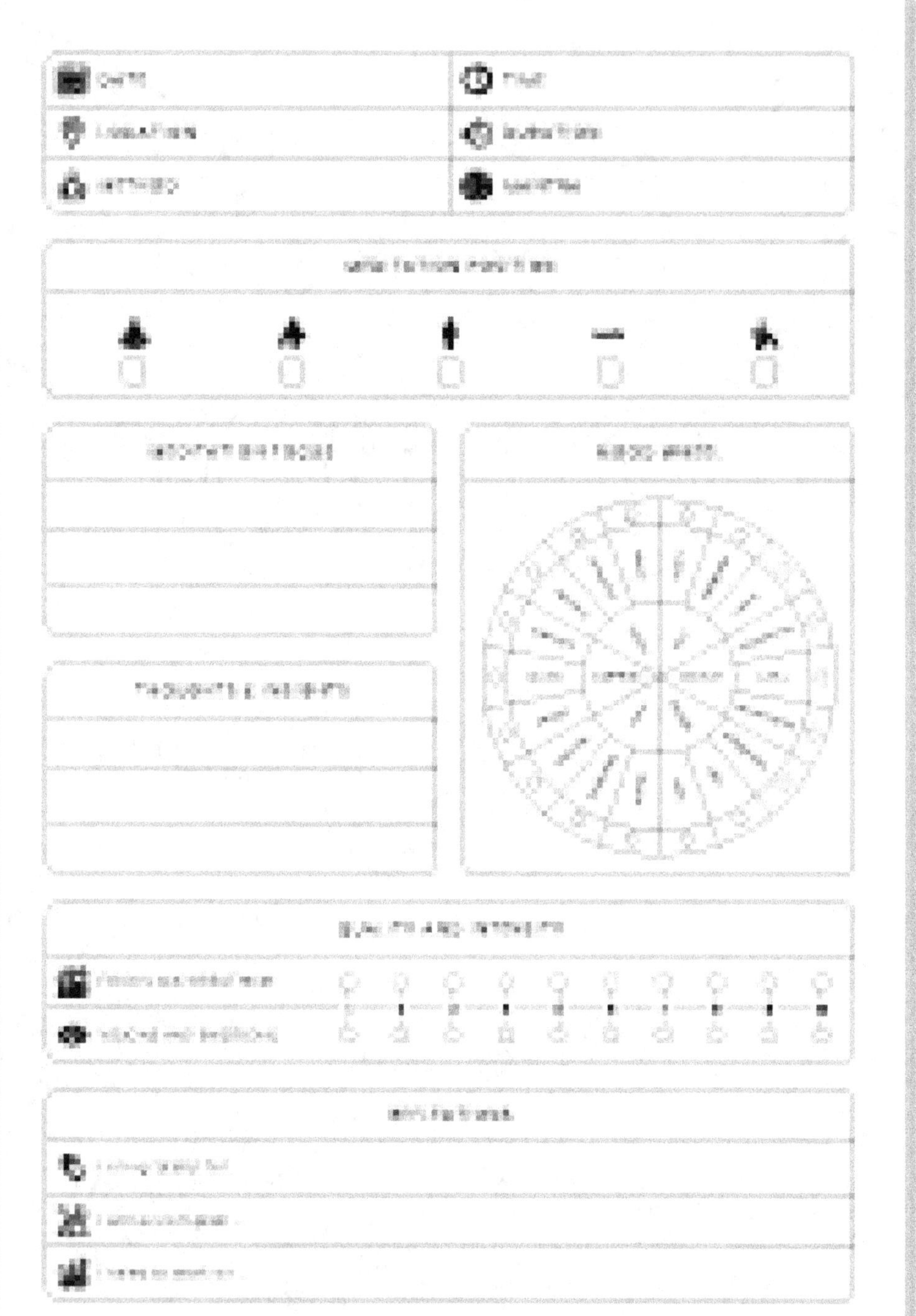

# MEDITATION DIARY

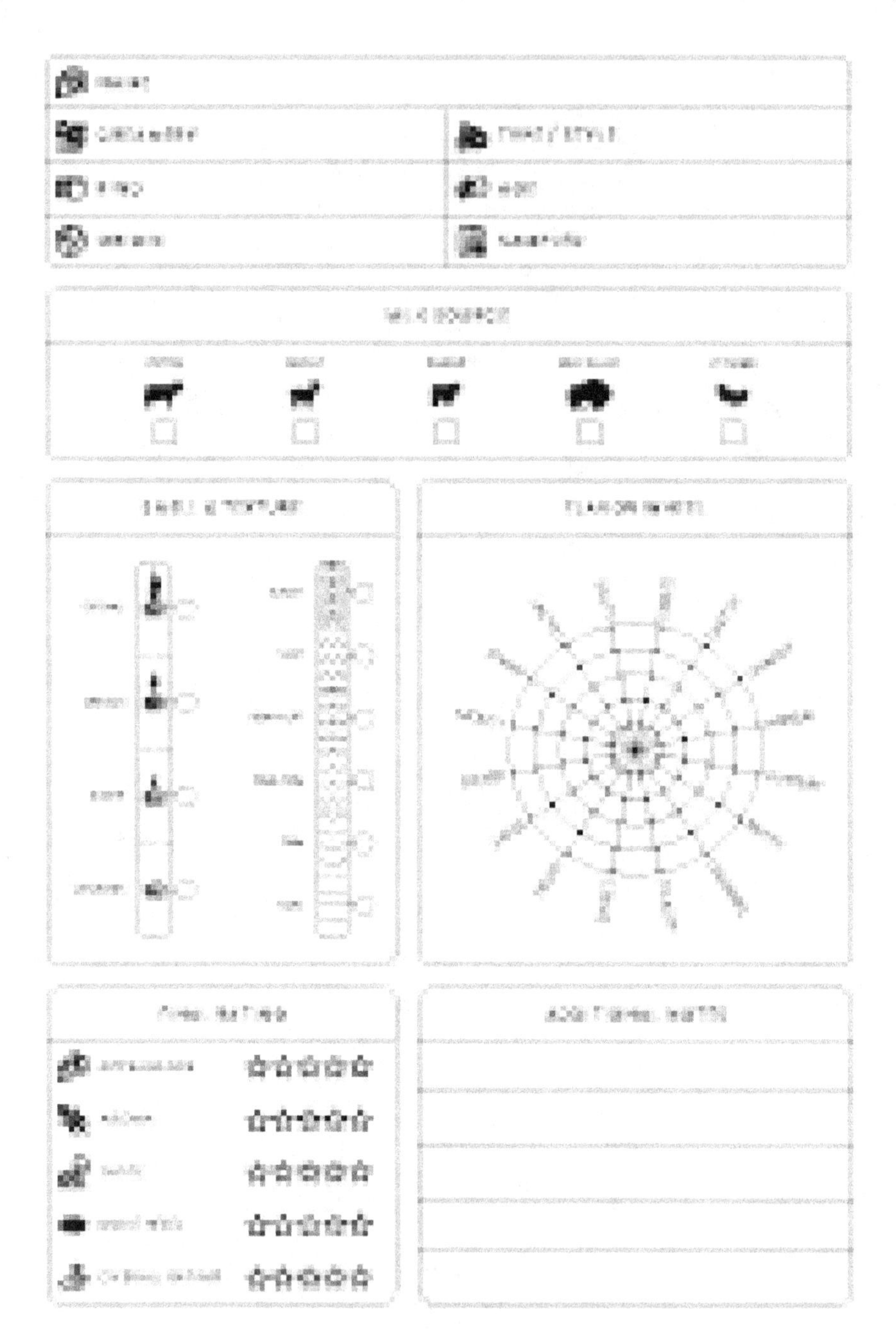

# CHEESE TASTE JOURNAL

www.ingramcontent.com/pod-product-compliance
Lightning Source LLC
Chambersburg PA
CBHW081427250726
48654CB00013B/1853